ISBN: 978-0-9930695-1-2

Copyright © Kay Channon 2017

The right of Kay Channon to be identified as the author of this work has been asserted in accordance with the Copyright, Designs and Patents act 1988 All rights reserved. This book is sold subject to the condition that it shall not, by way of trade or otherwise, be lent, resold, hired out, or otherwise circulated without the publisher's prior consent in any form of binding or cover other than that in which it is published and without a similar condition, including this condition being imposed on the subsequent purchaser

Set in Baskerville Old Face

Published by

Bardic Media, Unit 601,

10 Southgate Road,

London N1 3LY

The Dark Side
of Light

Kay Channon

For all those who continue to listen to the deafness of the turning world. May these words bring you peace through thoughtful pain.

I could not Speak, and my eyes failed, I was neither

Living nor dead, and I knew nothing,

Looking into the heart of light, the silence.

The Waste Land - T S Eliot

About the author

Kay Channon wrote her first poem at the age of eight, which was awarded a local poetry prize, and in 2008 she received the Hargreaves Award for English. She is currently studying poetry in the context of disability culture, cyberculture, and the formation of hybrid identities, as part of her PhD at the University of Chichester. She enjoys reading philosophy as well as feminist literature.

Born at 26 weeks, and having to deal with lifelong health issues arising from this, Kay says, "*The Dark Side of Light* drifted in and out of an abyss which spoke of an unavoidable silence. As I became more familiar with this space, I realised there was so much more to listen to than the inaudible beat of my heart..."

To my friends at Harbour Poets

Contents

My Words are My Voice   - 9

The Dark Side of Light   - 11

Infinite Beauty   - 22

Letters   - 24

Dissolve   - 26

Tide   - 28

Silent Speak   - 30

Hope   - 32

Buzzing   - 34

Passage   - 36

Fire   - 43

Sea   - 45

Laughter   - 47

Candle Flame   - 50

Dear Angel   - 52

Void   - 54

Masquerade   - 56

Doves   - 58

Broken Crow   - 60

Stars	- 62
Musings	- 64
Room	- 65
Kiss of Death	- 67
Near Drowning	- 69
Brittle	- 72
April Rain	- 75
For The poem	- 77

My Words Are My Voice

My words are my voice
A choice as natural as breathing
Sitting, repeating
And by nature deceiving

I am lying
On a bed
It is my head that talks

Sometimes blindness is the greatest gift
It lets the darkness speak
To slip between the unseen and scream
There is no rhyme for this

Sublime space?
If only...
Sinking through the flaws in your skin,
Your bones dissolving in a poet's shadow fading

Made worthy, unworthy, worthy, unworthy, worthy more and more
What is this for?

I appeal to the listener who thinks they've heard it all
by the blink of my eyes
This image talks indeed
Shaking in its unsteady shell shackled,
But I am not its reflection
I am the silence within the unspoken
The spoken aloud, not alive

Cut down, edited, repressed
Made strong (or so they think)
In the name of art
Or speech that may be understood in more than clarity's tongue
Stuttering so quietly in its searching
You won't even know that it's gone...

The Dark Side of Light

1.

When people ask me I say
I am busy
I am busy with nothing
writing nothing
doing nothing
sitting inside, and outside, of nothing

being nothing
I am nothing

walking an invisible path which everyone thinks they can see
but they are looking at someone else
"Look here's the edge" they say then disappear
locked inside my own body
I search for words, new words
something to take me beyond this stalemate
nothing moves me

I am not depressed

silence is not sorry, it is not a sign, nor a broken sigh

it's a process of thinking.

2.

They say she never talks any more

she must be depressed

she likes to sit and think

there was a man who in the passing of an hour gave her one sacred forbidden kiss

"Tell me what's in your head?"

the first tears of the month fell

she summoned all her strength to inhale, to hold this moment

she knew it would not last...

I think it goes beyond words

he continues to press her, begging,

"Please, tell me what's in your head?"

you won't like the answer

she wishes they could go back to the entrance again

back to a time when Sartre was just an object of reading on the nightstand

he was the only one who didn't mock

he understood but he would not understand this

she was not good enough with the words or with her heart to ask him to stay

and time was far too clever

they were both made to love and destroy each other in one single moment

and there it was

the greatest, most passionate and most hateful thing never to have happened

"Do you love me?"

"Yes. But I know it's not enough"

"Why didn't you say before?"

"It's not in me to hurt you like that people shouldn't belong to people they should be free"

"I know you want to be free"

there's so much light

the door clicks

he leaves

3.

Today wants to break

today wants to cry

today wants to disappear

today starts weeping

everything weeps

4.

Ten days, ten lives, ten whispers

none of them mine

standing in the rain feeling anything but wet

a shadow for my life to my life in my life

speak a speech for something gone by

don't worry that you don't know how it should sound

there doesn't seem to be an end to this space and that scares me

everything joins only to be broken again and again

inside a severed head that will not stop screaming

"I need you to stop screaming"

"I'm worried"

invisible tears tread upon a face – the face that is giving up

silence kills the soul, wiping away tears as the body withers

what I want to say is so much more than what is in this pen

this is only half the story

I wish I could give you more

I wish you could see the other half

the one that blocks out everything

O teach me how to cry again

so that this might mean something

and stand for itself

5.

"Do you know God?"

"I..."

"Do you know God?"

"I've felt angels before but I've never been that good with religion. I get too distracted and caught in other things I think I believe too much in people and freedom to be good at religion

knowing God shouldn't isolate it should liberate you know? I think if there was a way I could know God without religion then that would be okay to be honest I think he has far more important things to attend to right now"

"Say A-men"

"A...wait...why not A-woman?"

6.

My life my life my line my life

what am I doing?

all for letters, all for words

all for who?

for what?

I know not.

I hope not.

I know not.

I know hope?

all I am are words on a page in a space to be read by no one

the world's most patient patient

Mr (who is more than twice my age) would you like to come through please

Mrs (who is even older than him) would you like to come through please

"Just to let you know the clinic is an hour behind but we may catch up".

my life my life my line my life wasting in this void?

he said he was proud

only took him nine thousand four hundred and ninety days (approximately) and one near death experience

believe it or not that was the first time

absent

how can someone be so marked in your blood

and yet be so absent so blind so...

"Excuse me. Would you like to come through..."

7.

Happy happiness you piss me off

everyone expects you without reason or boundary

they expect me to wear you all the time

what if I want to wash you?

I can't usually wear the same clothes for more than three days

(unless I am very sick)

go somewhere else

I'm bored of you

we are officially at the low point

I've started to talk about my bedroom carpet again

it's one of the few things I actually feel comfortable talking about that isn't in books I've read...

my brain stutters and goes blank

"I want you to close your eyes and visualise a person who you would believe unconditionally"

"Slavoj Žižek"

"That's an unusual answer"

I had succeeded in educating my therapist

and that week we escaped far too many Freudian clichés

8.

It settled on a flower

I forget the colour but I remember the butterfly

yes

its wings opening and closing in a gentle rhythm

tapping together in silence

one, two, three, four, five

if only I could count time like that

and pass through life with such grace and beauty

but I have no wings - just a stupid brain and tired limbs

"Other people get sick you know"

where is the line?

when is it enough?

I am in the orchard again

I hug the branch close to my heart and trust it to support me

close to freedom and closer then I have ever been to the sun

winter

"And what have you been doing for all these hours?"

"I've been in my room, reading"

"No you haven't"

and so burnt the fire...

9.

Nanny's brave little soldier

has such a temper

Nanny's brave little soldier

is good in school but forgets to say thank you

Nanny's brave little soldier

loves to read but cannot spell

Nanny's brave little soldier

was scared when he put his hand over her mouth and pressed down hard and cried and cried when they wouldn't stop pushing needles into her legs

she was nine and very much awake

"Why are you doing this to me. I hate you"

Nanny's brave little soldier does not want to be brave

10.

Space is not great when it does not speak

when it sits idly by and watches

waiting...

for the next tick of the clock

the next breath

the next sunset

"Where are you then?"

"Up and down"

blackness intertwined with white squares

flashing flashing

this is bad, very very bad

flashing flashing

she, it, him, them, then, they,

the crackle of a distant phone call

not how I imagined...

no

this is not what I imagined at all

now the squares are bending their edges

threatening to turn into something else

something other...

please please don't.

not now

not like this

this is not what I imagined at all...

Infinite Beauty

One broken body
a mind forever free
encoding life's patterns
of infinite beauty

A need to trace the illogical
inside a web of light
hand in hand with the shadows
that follow infinite beauty

Imagination unfolding forever
dividing the limitless realms
an answer which explains nothing
the victim of infinite beauty

Knowledge breeds confusion
though time cannot be changed
a face of a thousand scars reflects
the pain of infinite beauty

A helpless cry of ignorance

obscured by endless silence

though I am deaf to the world

I see beyond

the eyes of infinite beauty

Letters

Across the empty plane

Sits an empty coffee cup of stagnant promises.

It is flat and almost impossible to see.

Why does time creep around when others are waiting?

Fear, boredom, or maybe just embarrassment?

Isolation?

A wretched figure.

A man without sympathy

The only living phantom.

Today I feel like writing,

But that's nothing new.

This time I will seek to write meaning rather than feeling.

Today I will write.

Shapes and servitude?

No.

They are not sisters.

They cannot join hands.

Life -

A sketch without a model

But we can move if we want to.

A need for safety cannot always match with love.

A letter can be torn or returned to the recipient

Closed and sealed.

A stamp.

A shout.

A scream.

A light.

A cycle.

An empty cage.

Dissolve

Strength dissolve
take me down
I have no penny for the ferryman
so I float un-destined to my fate

Light a candle
but be blind to the flame
speak to the silence
and listen from its shell

Look not for words but feel their wave
there is no longer a there or then, just an 'is'
that has passed
torn through time; something which we all wait for
something that fails us...

Memory a faceless phantom
scattered cards with endless incomplete numbers
one breath that does not and cannot answer itself

caught in a moment, unmoving, stepping in line with the next death

echoing – "Not this one"

in the absence of thee it is not your turn

Tide

Death is easy
it's the treading
the before and the after which is difficult.

The constant questioning
of the path, the turning point, the no return.

The wanting to show the right face to the faceless
exhaled and exhausted.

Stepping around and backward
toward a fractured future.

Each mouth moves so afraid of lies, that is all they can speak
over and over again
winding ticker tape around the universe,
our universe.

Click, trip, slip
through the cracks

try to make up the numbers

show your worth

You can only divide by yourself, not one.

Consumed by the tedium

wanting to feel the tide without getting wet

telling yourself; "I am a different kind of robot"

thinking you are better.

This colonised consciousness

invades the bloodstream

making the whole body believe,

making you stand

as the words of the world, this world,

collapse...

Silent Speak

speak so I may not see

the words leave your lips

speak without breath or sound

hold still our fragile glass portrait of a life

soon to be stolen

ask not why the dry sand tears and blood mix

scratching, scratching at the edge

the right grain is lost now and so is the eye that cries and curses

let it weep and let us speak not of the sound

do not trace the lie and say you know these footprints, these ashes, this heart

do not say you know anything of this

words without witnesses

the beat of a dream

the interlude of distance

so much interrupted silence

the kind that shows you nothing

making space for the wrong kind of meaning

hearing itself over and over

words will not solve this

language shall not swallow nor reduce it

we are elsewhere now

Hope

Hope is a name
nothing more
I must get to know it
shake it by the hand
I must get to know it.

The clocks answer each other
in an out of step chorus
as shadows grant an unhappy marriage on the wall.

O innermost music
stir me
so that my tomorrow is not missed
mistaken for today.

I must shake it
shake the hand of hope.

Time to walk towards the unforgiven
bitter mercy, forever bitter mercy

masquerading as pain upon pain
breath upon breath upon pain.

Hope takes a step
static like a stranger in the wind.

The clocks stop
my breath stops
matter becomes mind
mind becomes matter.

Hope screams and then
dissolves...

Buzzing

Swirling in a sea of despair
waves beating, beating
high pitch humming inside my head
Yes,
This is better than thinking.

Loose, free in my own sphere of illusion
cliché but wonderful
like a taste of ecstasy
higher, higher
I am higher.

My conscience says little
at least for now
maybe tomorrow it will speak.

Resistance? Pointless
when I am already there
distance is closer
much closer now...

Blissful solitary life?

I cannot control it

I cannot choose it

but I will embrace it.

Yes.

I enjoy this 'not thinking' state

I am in a quiet place

at peace...

Passage

1.

The world lies

laying still in a box of rainbow colours

untouched

The pulled threads of the clown towel my latest shroud

handprint upon handprint stacked then erased

regardless of the fall

in a thankless task yet to be completed

I am not the child foreseen

but a hybrid of many could-have-beens

a broken silhouette in the name of normal

2.

It all began with a photo – Big Ben

I could never understand how my teacher knew it was male

it was a slave to time yes

to me a very human problem

Midday frozen in its frame

next to my blank page

I had one hour to capture this midday as I saw it

a psychedelic scene was born

She stood steadfast

a goddess in the sunset sky

a lively mismatch of yellow, orange, and pink

holding midday with pride

in a mass of painted clouds without rain

Happiness greeted me in my task

I missed the heated arguments for brown, blue, and black as others reached for photo perfection

I concentrated on my world of purple

a world which I was soon taught to be inappropriate for a six year old

3.

I think the smell was part of the ruse

something which made you think of good clean fun

the warm waters a sly brittle anaesthetic for later pains

ready to cramp and twist through once dormant nerves

from sensation to fit and fit to sensation –

progress comes at a price

Kick faster, faster, don't slow down

my heart stuttered

I held my breath

knowing what awaited me on dry land was much worse

4.

The marriage of musk, dampness, and yet to weep spring rain

fed my joy

she was all I needed

Although not exclusive

I rested my head against her tousled mane and breathed in the dust cloud from her damp veined skin

identity merged

we were the same

Trust followed without hesitation

wrapped inside of a second

with sight no longer a variable and time less than an afterthought we could do more than walk together –

we could fly

5.

On reading his message my heart became lead

I, the creator of a lie so white, so infinite

the core of my own crumbling world

with smiles upon smiles reflected back to me in a looking glass half the ideal size

6.

It was the sound of my sister

my ears were playing the latest simplified choral arrangement

the soundtrack of years six, seven, and most of eight

when you are a child you can make most mutterings into rhymes and rhymes into songs

forgetful catchy rhymes and happy songs

I could not do this with my sister's mutterings

they made her so happy

over time it just became 'the way things were'

as for love - it was never affected

7.

Someone gets out the photographs from the draw that sticks

remembering brings a sickness unique to the soul

greener than green and blacker than the deepest grey

You reach with hands you used to control

thinking of the tell-tale crease

through the web of absurdity surrounding the question of separate bedrooms

you consider the fold

in a world that expects and accepts 'normality' – the idea of other children

Half the pack sits behind the negatives

your stomach relaxes –

you exhale

as the clock bares the silent realisation that the photos they are interested in never existed anyway

8.

I wished with all my heart that he had been my father

that I could animate the clay

that he could see me now without the safety of the cliché

or the vices that I knew would destroy him

I wished that very particular way he kept saying 'I love her'
could change the situation

and stop me wanting his empty kisses

As a teenager I thought I had found the answer

and brought a rosary -

(despite being raised as a protestant)

Still the hair filled the bin

clinging to the scissors

as you looked at that one everlasting self-made scar

worthless, useless, endless

still

9.

Dear stranger I am yet to meet

I think I am full of sin, so full of sin

I went to Mass and I was afraid - not because of my misunderstanding, because it was underground

during the blessing I felt nothing

am I full of sin? So full of sin

I should have learnt their songs

I didn't think they would be so different -

we were all there for the same God after all

my mouth moving in soundless motions trying to give the impression I was living

as my wrong doing grew bigger

10.

The rains turned to floods and the floods turned to tears

for the wrong reasons, selfish reasons

and for the end

Fire

White watermarks scar ice pricked skin
A broken mess not fit for display
The fire burns no more

Hospital use only
Imprinted on the poet
Through silence broken by less than a whisper
That last absent pen a wishful forgotten curse

The need to write a different ending moaning
Overtaking the droning heart trying to beat and sing to the fire
That fire – my fire
Its ashes distant, not wanting to join the contagious bond
Cardboard sheets folded back in rigid finality

The fire, now fleeting,
Exposes every retch
Cough spasm and convulsion

With a throat unable to swallow

And lungs barely moving

There is no water – no need to speak of life or the life of the fire

There is no song, accept, perhaps, something with a ring around it

A touch cannot comfort this waxwork

It's dying hour framed by frigid solitude

As unmoving hands start to reverse

In the fading light of the fire

Sea

The wind told me to come

if anyone asks that's what I'll say

as I stand on the edge of this salty cliff

dripping

I shall say I was forced

hypnotised by nature's song

paralysed by deafness

they will not know this was meant

meant with such purpose my heart reversed and reverted to silence

beautiful, unwavering, uncompromising, silence

What did the youngest daughter do?

she came, she saw and suffered so beautifully

a tragic accident maybe

they wouldn't understand

They want real people with real ideas

but they know nothing of reality

nothing of pain or injustice
there is only love and pain in the dust
fragmented love and relentless pain
as the sea screams to the end
we cannot be friends my friend
alas, we cannot be friends

So drain my blood and stop me crying
as the sky climbs down to meet us

Laughter

I laugh because I feel it's polite
I laugh because I don't want you to know how offended I am
I laugh because I am afraid
I laugh because in the street, everyone stares

I laugh because you have no idea what you are saying
I laugh because there is no cure or time to explain
I laugh because I want you to know I can take a joke
I laugh because you bore me so much

I laugh because I don't want you to assume I'm mute
This pain could last years
I laugh because they said "Don't you want children?"
I laugh to block out the memory of him saying he hates this

I laugh because most people just focus on what's on the outside
I laugh because I've heard it all before
Because I don't want to feel powerless
I laugh because I am speechless

I laugh because that's what most people do when they are 'coping'

I laugh because it's just another needle, another pill,

I laugh because I miss him

I laugh because no matter how hard I try he just isn't interested

I laugh because it is important

I laugh because I think I was in love with her but was too young to realise it at the time

I laugh to try to forget how sincere he sounded when he said -

"I don't care about that stuff. It's your mind I'm in love with"

I laugh because most people hate silence

I laugh because, in this place, death doesn't seem to matter

I laugh when I need to forget that he hit her and he kicked her more than once

I laugh because people throw the word hope around like it's the answer to everything

I laugh because it's better than crying

I laugh because I almost died

I laugh because I survived

I laugh because I want to feel happy

I laugh because I forget it makes me out of breath

I laugh because I don't want to break down

Because I don't want to hurt your feelings

I laugh because unfortunately, that's what it takes, to get most people to listen

Candle Flame

Oh sweet oblivion
where is your song?
I want to hum your tune in the darkness

Unfold, unfold into starless blue
my comfort
the only thing I can count on in this world

Oh come, come away
away from the heart of the candle flame
I know what it feels like to burn
the melting wax shall marry my skin

No scars, no imperfections
a figure without purpose
without interpretation
made to be anything

Without a mould of the self
hold...

For we are what we are
closed and sealed for others to beat
sorry souls in a mosaic of pain
looking for utopian lies to make us smile

Dear Angel

Why does your harp weep blood?
singing the notes of the same song
over and over
what is higher than hope?
is there a passage for those who don't pray?

Dear angel
why are you so still?
your stone-like skin forever set in dread
your eyes do not cry for forgotten reasons
they cry for a past future only you can see

The dead have their reward
peace, a place, a time outside of ours
so much to say with no one to listen
made deaf by trampling feet
now they speak a different language

Dear angel
I shall shake your unforgiving hand

and wait for the passing dawn

and hope the sun will rise

making me blind to blindness

so that a new day can break

then with your hand

I shall dance

Void

Such an empty head
the eye holes possessing distant stares
their only purpose to dissect the furthest nothing
without seeing...

There are birds around me
I do not hear them sing
locked inside this paper dream
made to be crushed,
recycled by the day

The sun has made again
a 'me' 'you' and an 'I'
they stand divided at the edge
as the head rolls on
like a lost pilgrim

Lines above
lines below
trying to show the answer

it does not want to be found

Pure, colourless, less than itself
it can teach us more than the heart could ever echo
but the head is bored blind and tired

Masquerade

Merging canopies
brightness without sun
airless air, taunting shadows,
a masquerade without reason.

Time is becoming too friendly
too close for comfort,
a hand to the useless airless air
"There is no need to cry."

A release from the known unknown
from the impossible,
amidst the airless air
back, falling in line with the familiar.

Identity fading,
lost,
replaced by weakness,
by emptiness; and more and more airless air.

The forest is unkind.

you cannot creep around its creepers.

you cannot deny its nature.

or break its airless air.

One chance remains,

a chance to fight

to masquerade.

This time with reason

a head, a heart

And a life.

Doves

A pure tapestry of white

Clothing the eyes of the innocent

Purified by beams of sun

Milky smooth

Forever moving

My seat: the balcony

In limbo between place and place

Longing to fly –

To find my home, my mate

Leaning forward

Nose pressed against the edge of their sky

A passage to a different life inhaled

But air moves you

You do not move the air

You cannot choose the impossible hidden by such beauty such perfection

You are not part of this union

The gentle coo hums to the darkness of the eyelids
A reminder of distance
A scarred mark of sorrow between my language and theirs
The near spoken word suspended
Soon to be unravelled by too much thinking

They are further now
A smaller fading dream
Like floating rice paper
A hope of horizon above the iron bar
Shaping what will come to pass in the mind's eye only

Broken Crow

They do not see the crow weep

Its starving heart shrivelled up in black ribbons

Hoping and dipping for a morsel of food

The eyes black and darting

It is not capable of tears

Just a strangled cry mistaken for a squawk

Searching for its missing companion in a mass of feathery ink

The slapping and poking brings blood

A slow drip of meaningless time

Making a map on the grass

The route of a hated hopeless being

Driven by its empty kills

The victim of misshapen identity

Twisting, darting, and squawking still

No one will honour this fearless warrior

Common pest

Common noise

Common nuisance they shall say

His last stand will go unnoticed

Stars

The stars speak a soft low hum
a lullaby for the unwoken unspoken night
here lies not the rhyme
nor the undying light
but something more

A reflected beauty of the unknown
a distant acknowledgement of the abyss
they sing not of wars
Or once bright futures

The top of the poet's head is nothing but a ring of fading light
the scratch of the pen mistaken for the reversing wind

Witness to words at their feet
which cannot be read, returned, or exchanged

"My name is no one
There is no need to count its syllables"

Happy orphans, they blink, not to the night

nor its sister sun

but for the stranger who does not see

for the child who does not wish

and for the father who searches for his son

in the blanket of time

masquerading as the sky

Musings

Many things have become about grief –
grief and absent noises
sadly tuneful in the shadow of the sun
screaming...

The problem being that grief does not come with tears
or strange habits
(they have always been there)
nor under the protected comfort of sentimental objects
but inside the painted perfection of a Russian doll.

Memories hidden, stacked away
inside the surface beauty of a carved face
the silent metaphor removed now a scratch mark in the brain.

But I cannot write of these things
at least not in a way language can measure
if I could then I would be a poet.

Room

I think about the rain

wishing it would penetrate the windows

the drops cross each other like busy train commuters

marking the panes with their impatient trails

there are too many to count but still I try

taking it as a comfort that there are more,

more of them than the hanging odd ninety-one square ceiling tiles that won't sit still

Mum always said –

"Don't go out in the rain you shall catch your death"

I never thought a statement could carry so much irony

I examine the watermark on the dim night light bulb

it must have rained at least once in this room

rained with something other than the flow of human tears

there must be a way in

I took the smallest hope then that there must be an exit, a way out

The rain now restless carries with it the wind

disrupting the flow of artificial air con which decreases to a low hum

in tune with my heart

Kiss of Death

Lay down your head

Let the screams ring

Drowning, drowning in the white water

The absent blood of another on the bed sheets

The marks of the ghost gone before you

A Stone like stillness

So cold you forget feeling

Half formed thoughts plague the brain

Maybe nothing will stay this time

The bleep of disappointment the only fanfare

No angel chorus

No feverish montage

Just a body and a ceiling

One body

One ceiling

She wills his voice to return

Convinced this is the moment

He does not come

Not even in her imagination

Love takes the shape of doubt

Rising and falling in place of its missing piece

Maybe eight is the answer?

It's as good a number as any

Nothing separates nothing

She makes her own silent lullaby

And sings it to death

Wrapped in a blanket of bleach

These tears are for time only...

Near Drowning

Dear God

let me drown

torn down and tired

let me drown

Reaching for a new nothing

a day without a daybreak

without light

without sound

let me drown

In a silence so still it mourns its own shadow

time has played the same tone for too long

far too long

tears made so unreal

even sadness cannot speak of them

bleeding the poison of a now selfish soul

making their waves

time to drown

Nothing,

nothing worth saving

just limp limbs

nothing

just nothing

Up crops the question "Why was I saved?"

again and again

"What should I do now?"

"Count your blessings or be cursed my child"

A stamp of importance placed upon my head

When the world is better than this place

Is it time to drown?

They took me to the top

the top of your house

a trip – they said

"A change of scene"

every teenager's dream

I played the role of a needy house guest

(not my role of choice)

The hand shake never came
there was no time to settle in
wrapped in a blanket of sterile whiteness, soap, tubes and lines

A younger, more naïve self
cried in weak whispers –
"Please God, don't let me die"

Now he cannot return...

Brittle

I want to make friends with my body

but we cannot speak in this space of pain

this light of shade

this darkness inside of darkness

You, in the mist of this fading

dwarfed by the eyeless horizon

catatonic, speechless

facing forward

The static is too loud

we cannot hear each other

tormented by the possibility of time joining time

in a sense without sense

Unreachable

Anger eclipsed by weakness and weakness eclipsed by poetry

hands tracing the edge of definition

it cannot contain itself

and in joining others

becomes a failed Monet

a blurred window without a reflection

There are so many things of which I wish to speak

the silence is winning

soon to be my blanket

waiting to find comfort in this disorder

looking for a corner to drop my paperweight

to mark the end of this chapter

I worry not for the end of the story

it can direct itself

but for what happens in its making

For that which is remembered and held in the wake of absentminded truth

In my blissful ability to forget

others will find answers

a problem indeed – As 'I' is always different to 'her'

always changing...

Is there a moon on earth?

is there a place for those looking for love in other things?

not in the face of another

nor in the fragile frame of nature

but in something ever-lasting, infinite, immune to the flow of human blood?

A heartbeat

a necessity

a breath underwater

These angels aren't from God

I know not their names

only their notes outplaying sorrow

floating on a stave in the uncharted wind

My own high pitch chimes mix with their song

not wishing to count or measure the sands of time

but to reach a place of the living

April Rain

Sing to me sweet April rain
Protect me from the burning sun
Cleanse me of my past
So I can step beyond the border

Sing to me sweet April rain
Lift my fever of hate
Wrap me in your caress
And take a walk with me

Sing to me sweet April rain
Lead me to the circle
Tie my hand to yours
So we can dance

Sing to me sweet April rain
Let me sleep tonight
Make me a melody of love and light

Sing to me sweet April rain

Hold me close

Please sing to me sweet April rain

Sing to me forever

For The Poem

I sit by my bedside

Watching the pale body so still and quiet

I lean forward and whisper, "What should I take with me? It might be a long trip"

The eyes blink but do not speak

I am left staring at an empty suitcase

I look inside and smell the familiar rose scent of Nan

I smile

I was being overcautious – She never took a bag, she never had time

Not even the borrowed kind

But is she happy? Bored?

Maybe. She liked to keep busy

The body trembles then

I rearrange the covers

It's always good to leave the room the way you wish to find it, just in case

The eyes gesture to the bookshelf

I frown

"How am I meant to pick? There are so many"

The body remains still, I sigh

My hand hovers over *The Neverending Story* –

Not wanting to be cliché at such an important time I pause

Maybe I don't need a story that's already written

Maybe I can write something new

The yellowish parchment now flutters restlessly in the suitcase

Scattering half written half completed pages over the seat of the carpet

Each one clings to an unreachable invisible dream

The body in the bed coughs breathless and irritated

"Sorry I'm making you tired. I'll be finished soon"

I close the window to stop the breeze from scattering the pages any further

Then sit crossed legged on the carpet

Tracing the worn out lines with my fingertips

"Do you remember that walk?"

 Silence

"I'm sure you do. Down to the river with only jelly shoes on my feet

It was hot. Hot enough that the other children were standing in the water in their shorts

Mum stood me up at the edge of the shallowest water after I begged her

I wanted to see if the water made the glitter in my jelly shoes sparkle –

It felt nice"

Cough

The hand shakes

The water spills

The body moans staring at the empty glass

I reach inside the suitcase for a small towel to mop up the water

The eyes glazing begin to tear

"Don't worry it'll be dry soon enough"

Then I realise - placing the damp towel on its forehead

The eyes relax a little

The next sound is not the click of the door but a high-pitched scratching as chalk marries the wall

We both flinch

Hating the necessity of the task

But these things must be thought through with care

There is no point going anywhere when you don't have a map

"I'm sorry to ask but I think I need your advice"

The chalk now a stump freezes mid-stroke

The body groans

The chalk crumbles

I sweep up the dust

Creating a white comb-like mountain on top of the ready to overflow bin

I push the remaining rubbish down

The body twitches

I stand in front of the chalk covered wall

There are so many possibilities

Spaces in between spaces

I was going to get lost

The empty water glass wobbles

I hold it steady sweating a little

"Why are you still here?

The question falls flat as I try to swallow

"Why are you still here?"

"I have to be" I say

As the choking and coughing gets louder

"But why?"

I shut the empty suitcase and slide it back under the bed

The room feels cold suddenly

I check the window

Finding it closed I cross the room and crawl into bed

Pull up the covers

Wrap my arms gently around the shivering body and softly whisper

"For the Poem"